Ford and Etal
Glimpses from bygone days

FORD VILLAGE.

Etal Castle.

Introduction

FORD and Etal Estates lie within the ancient kingdom of Northumbria, a unique and beautiful place.

Its history began centuries ago when men and women from prehistoric times made these northerly lands their home. Survival then depended on their skills as hunters and farmers.

They made progress, creating tools, learning the art of copper and bronze smelting. But there were always forces outside their control.

Fearsome Viking invaders crossed the North Sea to plunder and pillage.

In medieval times merciless battles were waged on this soil between armies from England and Scotland.

It was here, at Flodden, on the 9th September 1513, that vast swathes of mud turned blood red as King James IV of Scotland and 10,000 of his men were hacked, stabbed and battered to death in just two hours.

For hundreds of years this area was a gangland where feuding families and neighbours raided, blackmailed and murdered.

Where once men and women had been skilled in farming, centuries of turmoil turned the countryside into an agricultural wasteland. Thousands starved.

The history of Ford and Etal is about the struggles successive generations of men and women have faced here each day simply to find enough food to live, protect themselves from their enemies and find shelter from the elements.

And while a life of hunger and hardship was all too often the lot of the majority, we look also at the owners of Ford and Etal. These few have enjoyed fabulous wealth, privilege and power, but these pleasures were tempered for some by heartbreak.

The stories Ford and Etal and its people have to tell are compelling. This book presents glimpses of their, and our, past.

Survival: Iron Age farmers harvest their crops

Invasion: A woodcut of a Viking longboat

Battleground: A depiction of the brutal fighting at Flodden

A hard day's labour: Victorian farmworkers in the fields

Grandeur: Ford Castle in the 19th century

Eight thousand years of history

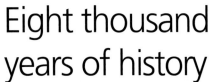

SINCE Stone Age times, about 8,000 years ago, men and women have raised their children among the low hills and valleys around Ford and Etal.

People lived simply, first as hunters and then as farmers. They tended crops of grain and vegetables and kept animals for food, clothing and labour. They rejoiced in seasonal celebrations and the excitement of bartering with rare passing pedlars.

Their children played with toys made from wood and stone shaped into animals, just as many still do today.

It was a self-sufficient peasant life and it continued for centuries.

Then from overseas came the Vikings, their wooden dragon ships bringing terror to the shores of North East England. They wanted loot and the undefended monasteries with their silver chalices, gold crosses and bejewelled books were soft targets.

The raids started at the priory on the small island of Lindisfarne in 793AD and sent shockwaves through the country, beginning an era of violence that would last, on and off, for more than 200 years.

The Viking raiders were ruthless, killing anyone in their way. The tall yellow-bearded men from Scandinavia fought with a bloodthirsty frenzy, 'like mad dogs or wolves', says one of their own chroniclers. Their ferocity was legendary.

The Vikings raided deep into the countryside returning home with their plunder before the autumn gales began. Then they began to winter in the north-east as well as Yorkshire, Norfolk and the Midlands. In 865 AD a full army arrived and stormed through the country taking three of the English kingdoms – Northumbria, East Anglia and Mercia – before finally attacking the remaining Anglo-Saxon stronghold of Wessex in the south.

There, the opposition to the Vikings was led by King Alfred the Great. He drove them from most of their English conquests in a long and desperate war. The Saxons regained most of their old territory and formed the first unified English kingdom. Anglo-Saxon England with a population of just over a million was created.

Rural life: Women tending sheep, an illustration from the Luttrell Psalter manuscripts. (c) All Rights Reserved. The British Library Board. Licence Number: NOREYE01

THE DUDDO STONES

FOR centuries the dramatic Duddo stone circle, just north of Etal, has formed part of the landscape of this area.

These five huge stones were quarried, carved with decorations, and hauled into a circle about 4,000 years ago.

What were they for? Historians believe the stones were most likely part of a Bronze Age burial site. Bones and charcoal have been discovered in the ground.

Monuments like these, which must have taken so much effort to build, reveal how important it was to bury the dead ceremoniously. These tombs were a link to a community's ancestors.

There are stone circles throughout the country such as that at Stonehenge which tells us of the uniformity of religious worship at the time.

The Duddo Stones are sometimes called the 'Singing Stones' because of way the wind whistles through their grooved surfaces.

Funeral: How an ancient burial site may have looked and (above) the Duddo Stones

THE MYSTERY OF ROCK-ART

THE creative, intellectual and spiritual life of prehistoric men and women in this northern land is revealed by ancient and mysterious stone carvings.

This rock-art was created by Neolithic and Early Bronze Age people from about 4,000 to 1800 BC.

More than 1,000 eaxmples have been discovered in Northumberland and one of the most significant is at Roughting Linn, close to Ford.

This is thought to be the largest carved rock in northern England with designs of circles, rings and hollowed cups. Researchers believe it dates back to the Neolithic Age, more than 4,000 years ago.

There are many theories about the role and meaning of rock-art, which is found throughout the world. Research is ongoing.

Some may have played a role in ceremonies such as funerals; perhaps it had spiritual significance. Or, other rock-art sites might have had a more practical purpose, perhaps as signposts or to mark out territory.

While its meanings have become lost in time, rock-art shows us that our long gone ancestors had logic, thoughts and passions as real as ours today. Rock-art is a direct record made by ancient people themselves, of the world they lived in and how they understood it.

Mysterious: Carvings on a boulder at Roughting Linn

THE ORIGINS OF FORD

LINDISFARNE Priory, just 14 miles away, was established by monks from the Scottish island of Iona in 635 AD.

The missionary Aidan had been sent there to help King Oswald of Northumbria restore his heathen Kingdom to Christianity.

Lindisfarne went on to became one of Europe's most holy sites, as well as a centre of ecclesiastical learning and scholarship which attracted many visitors.

Those travelling between the monasteries at Lindisfarne on the east coast and Iona on the west had to wade through the River Till and it is believed the village of Ford originated at the crossing point.

Journey: A depiction of how travelling monks may have looked in the Middle Ages

A hard life

LIFE in Anglo-Saxon England was short and brutal. Little had changed despite the new political regime and peace of sorts between the Saxons and Vikings.

Parents struggled to feed their children and many babies died of malnutrition or disease.

While there are no records of village life at Ford and Etal during this time, we do know people lived in small communities that straggled along a main street or surrounded a large green, perhaps for protection.

Their homes, which they shared with their animals, were one-room chimneyless thatched cottages made of wattle and daub or logs.

The countryside they lived in would seem to us a very different land. Ancient forests covered much of the area. Villagers gathered fuel, caught game and collected acorns for their pigs. They cleared strips of scrub for crops.

Home sweet home: An Anglo-Saxon village

Water was rarely safe to drink in the 9th and 10th centuries and people would drink weak beer, or imported wine if they were wealthy enough. Mead made with honey was popular here. They ate bread, cottage cheese, milk and cured meats, supplementing their diet with wild fruits, nuts and honey.

Peasants were governed by Anglo-Saxon law, which was a sort of collection of unwritten tribal 'customs'. An aggrieved person could take their case to a local public assembly and the court might decide on a test to find out who was telling the truth.

For instance the accused might have to walk six paces clutching a red hot iron or plunge his hand into a pot of boiling water to take out a stone. If the wound healed in three days he was telling the truth. If it did not, his burned hand was the least of his troubles.

The year 1000 was a turning point in history. There was a population explosion throughout Europe and rulers looked to expand their lands. William, Duke of Normandy had his eye on England and had a claim to the throne as a second cousin to the childless King Edward the Confessor.

When William finally defeated the English at Hastings in 1066, the country's social structure was reorganised into a new feudal system.

For the peasants toiling in the fields around Ford and Etal however, little changed. They continued to work hard from dawn to dusk, unaware of any social evolution.

Back-breaking work: Reaping and binding sheaves of grain, an illustration from the Luttrell Psalter. (c) All Rights Reserved. The British Library Board. Licence Number: NOREYE01

CHRISTIANITY COMES TO NORTHUMBRIA

THE royal palace of Ad Gefrin at Yeavering, just six miles from Ford, is part of the story of Northumbria's conversion to Christianity.

It was home to the powerful northern kings and queens of early medieval England.

They included Edwin, who ruled over an area stretching from Scotland to Yorkshire. Like the Northumbrian kings before him, Edwin was a pagan. He, his courtiers, priests and henchmen, worshipped idols.

But marriage soon changed all that. Two years after he wed the devout Princess Aethelburg of Kent in 625AD, he converted to Christianity, then a relatively new religion.

Full of enthusiasm, Edwin brought Paulinus, the Roman missionary who had baptised him, to Ad Gefrin for a 36 day visit in 627AD.

The entire kingdom of Northumbria became Christian, although it was another six years before this conversion became permanent.

The palace of Ad Gefrin itself had been built some 45 years earlier, around 580AD, for another powerful leader – Ida, the Danish Angle chief. He invaded the north-east coast and established the kingdom of Bernicia, as Northumbria was then known.

It continued to be an important royal residence, but was twice attacked and destroyed. By the end of the 7th century, it had been abandoned and the wooden buildings were left to rot.

Power: The vast kingdom of Northumbria

Conversion to Christianity: King Edwin is baptised by Paulinus

The new lords of the manor

THE recorded history of Ford and Etal begins soon after the Norman Conquest.

William the Conqueror now ruled over all of England. He imposed a new system of government, dividing his land or fiefs between his loyal followers to enjoy and administer.

The payback for the king was a supply of men and arms from his nobles whenever he demanded them.

Earliest documents show the two estates of Ford and Etal, which were then separately owned, were gifted to the Norman nobility around 1100.

This feudal system bound the workers or vassals to the lord of the manor in exchange for his protection.

Odinel, for example, who built Ford manor house in 1282, was expected to carry out justice on his estate. He collected tolls and other taxes, and in return was obliged to maintain roads, bridges and defences and care for the poor.

We can only speculate about the lives of the illiterate peasants living and working on his land. There are, of course, no records or diaries. But daily life was tough and dominated by customs and duties.

The peasant had to work his lord's land as well as his own allotment. He had to hand over a share of all his produce, repair the walls of the castle, feed the lord's dogs in the hunting season and even strip his own bed if the master ran out of bedding for guests.

Pay up: A 16th century woodcut showing peasants delivering their tithes

We do not know if Odinel de Ford or the Manners family, who then owned Etal, were good feudal lords, but they certainly fulfilled their duty to the king. Both men turned their homes into fortresses and forced their peasants to become foot soldiers on demand.

This was a system that was set to last for centuries.

BORN TO RULE – THE FEUDAL SYSTEM

FEUDALISM was a total organisation of society in which every person had their place.

It was a system that maintained nobles were born to their state by divine disposition and had a duty to rule the commoners

In medieval feudalism this meant the lord was regarded as socially, economically and politically superior. The theory was that in return for his wisdom and care, his workers provided services such as free labour.

In practice this so-called bargain usually favoured the lord.

RAIDS AND REPRISALS

THE power struggle between England and Scotland blighted the north for more than 300 years.

The English-Scottish frontier, just three miles from Ford and Etal, was the dividing line between two nations fighting their separate causes.

From the late 13th century to the middle 1500s, the border lands, known as the Marches, bore the brunt of war after war.

Life was shaped by this almost incessant violence. As the Scottish and English armies marched, burned and plundered the countryside, people had to find a way of existing.

They could not cultivate crops or build solid homes; they had to be constantly ready to flee. People learned to live on their wits and, when necessary, outside the law. Families, from every social class, came to live on the proceeds of raiding,

For some, this way of life became the norm, war or not. To these men, known as Reivers, killing, feuding, looting and blackmail were everyday life. The borders had become a gangster's paradise

There is no doubt this long struggle between England and Scotland devastated many lives, but perhaps at no time did it seem more savage than during the brutal battle fought in 1513, close to Ford and Etal, at Flodden.

Gangsters' paradise: Scottish Reivers setting out to raid cattle across the border with England

Blood and mud. The hell that was the Battle of Flodden

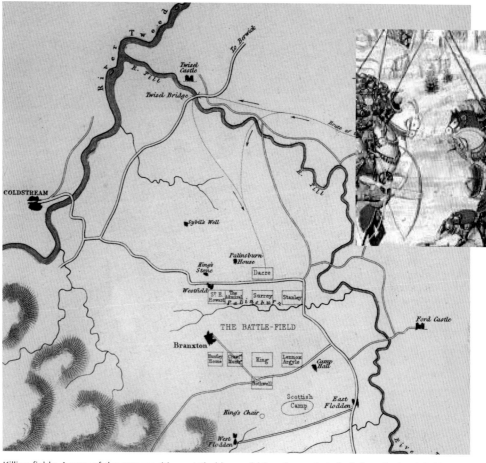

Killing fields: A map of the army positions at Flodden and (above) an artist's depiction of a battlefield

FOR several days in September 1513 James IV, the ambitious and nationalistic King of Scotland, unexpectedly dallied at Ford Castle as the largest Scottish army ever to enter England waited three miles away for his orders.

James had crossed the border several weeks earlier and stormed three other castles, including Etal, before taking Ford where the striking Lady Elizabeth Heron was home alone. The king had earlier imprisoned her husband in Scotland.

The Lady Elizabeth must have seemed delightful company after weeks on the road with his military commanders. So do her charms explain his baffling delay?

Certainly the 40-year-old king, who was married to Henry VII's daughter Margaret Tudor, was known to enjoy the company of women.

Or we could accept the theory that Elizabeth deliberately enticed James to stay with her, giving the English more time to prepare for battle. It is even suggested she might have

been a spy for Thomas Howard the Earl of Surrey, commander in charge of the English forces.

Whatever happened during those few days as he lingered at Ford enjoying the comfort of the best bedroom in the castle, this delay probably cost King James IV his life.

James left Ford on September 5th, setting fire to the castle as he went, and rode to his main camp at Flodden. By then however, the Earl of Surrey had marched hard to position his hastily-assembled troops north of

James's army cutting off any retreat into their homeland.

The size of the opposing armies can only be estimated. The Scots were left with about 30,000 after many deserted on the way down from Edinburgh, while the English had about 26,000 men.

The Scots were in a strong position on Flodden Hill, but on hearing that the English army had outflanked them and were marching on them from the north, James ordered his men to Branxton Hill.

It was a disastrous decision. It was on this rain-

Slaughtered: A portrait of James IV of Scotland, who died at Flodden

Best room: A depiction of how the king's bedroom may have looked during his stay at Ford Castle

lashed hillside on September 9th that a devastating story of brutal slaughter began to unfold.

James's motives for invading England in 1513 are complex. One theory is that he went to battle because of the Auld Alliance with Louis XII of France which promised mutual support should either be attacked by England. James's brother in law Henry VIII had recently invaded France.

Or, it may have been the French king's promised support for James's greater plan of a crusade against the Turks which convinced him to attack. Another idea is that this was just a quick skirmish onto English soil before the winter weather made an attack too difficult.

Whatever the reason, James's army was already hampered. His best gunners were with his navy helping the French. Both English and Scots had sophisticated artillery, but the English guns were lighter and better suited to the wet and slippery conditions. They picked off their enemy with deadly accuracy.

James catastrophically decided to abandon his position. He charged with hundreds of men and boys down the hill. They were raked by cannon fire and a rain of arrows. Those that reached the deep muddy bog at the bottom of the hill abandoned their sinking shoes to fight on in their sodden hose. Thousands were slain in these first minutes.

And in the hellish battle that followed, the Scots quickly discovered that their latest equipment, 20ft long Swiss pikes, were hopeless in hand to hand combat. The Englishmen hacked off the ends and chopped the great pikes into pieces. They were left defenceless.

In three hours some 14,000 men from both sides were cut to death by billhooks, swords and pikes. In that deep bog, where shouted orders competed with the screams of the injured, blood ran freely into the mud of Flodden.

James was killed along with his 19-year-old son Alexander. Only those who knew him well were able to identify his naked, mutilated body, his throat cut from ear to ear.

As for Lady Elizabeth, her husband William was released in exchange for Scottish prisoners taken at this final, poignant, medieval battle – the last time knights fought in armour, personal standards flying. Never again were swords, spears and arrows to be decisive weapons.

And never again would a British monarch die on the battlefield.

Battle over: A scene believed to show the victorious Earl of Surrey

THE WASTELAND OF THE 1600'S

THE decades following the Battle of Flodden were grievous years.

Nothing changed in the borders, even when James VI of Scotland came to the English throne after the death of Elizabeth I in 1603 although this Union of the Crowns brought about an uneasy peace.

It took this Border Commissioner's declaration in 1605 to signal the end of the border gangsters:

'If any Englishman steals in Scotland, or any Scotsman steal in England, any goods or cattels amounting to 12d, he shall be punished by death.'

In the first half of the 17th century, the border officers, some of whom were ex-reivers, enthusiastically went to work carrying out mass hangings, drownings and burnings of towers and houses. It was, bar the odd break-out of lawlessness, the finish of this area's troubles.

Left behind was an agricultural and economic wasteland.

Hunger and hardship in the fields

'FLATTER not yourselves with thoughts of long life,' wrote one chronicler of Northumberland in the early 1700s. For most men, women and children in the countryside lived in desperate poverty.

Few reached 40 because of chronic malnutrition with little but barley bread to eat.

The region's economy was devastated by centuries of fighting between Scotland and England. The countryside was mainly scrubland. Travellers generally regarded this part of the country as a wasteland. It was an 'entire desert . . . . fitted only for feeding cattle,' remarked one.

The economy slowly improved after the Acts of Union united the two countries in 1707 and eased restrictions on cross-border trading, but Northumberland remained behind the times. In 1770 an author touring the area wrote: 'A viler or more slovenly husbandry than theirs . . . can nowhere be found'.

It was only towards the end of the 18th century that the country-wide agricultural revolution reached this area.

The estate of Ford changed hands again and in 1754 the new owner Sir John Hussey Delaval took a great interest in new farming ideas and improving profitability.

He ended a feudal system of small holders subsisting on what they could produce and built 13 new bigger farms with rows of workers' cottages. He introduced modern ideas such as drainage, stock management, crop rotation and the most significant of all, land enclosure.

Before 1750, most farmland was divided into very large fields, often sub-divided into one-acre strips left fallow once every three years.

This system meant breeding stock lived close together and disease spread quickly.

It is most likely Sir John, like many other educated landowners, was greatly influenced by the famous agricultural experts of the day John Bailey and George Culley, who both lived near Ford. Bailey was a land agent, who redesigned the plough. Culley, a tenant farmer turned landowner, was an authority on innovative farming ideas.

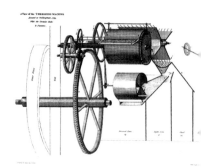

Latest design: A drawing of a threshing machine by John Bailey

Desperate: A portrait of a young mother and her three children foraging for fuel by A. Barlow

Together they wrote a report about agricultural practices in this area in 1793 for the newly-formed Board of Agriculture.

Thanks to their work and landlords like Sir John, who could see the profit such ideas could bring, Northumberland became a centre of technological improvement in the early 1800s.

❏ SIR John appears to be rather preoccupied with food in general. On June 25th 1807 these detailed instructions were sent to Ford Castle from Seaton Delaval Hall, Sir John's main Northumberland home, in preparation for his visit.

It orders that Phyllis is to 'pickle all the gerkins, and to slice and pickle all the large cucumbers. Also some onions and cauliflower and French beans. And to bottle a large quantity of gooseberries. As strawberries and other fruits come in she must preserve them and you are to procure for her sugars and whatever else may be necessary for so doing. You are to preserve all things of every sort that will keep till the family arrives'.

It adds that no one else is to pick anything from the garden without permission. His request for his first meal was '3 nice roasted chickens, a cold tongue, a cold forequarter of lamb with mint sauce, cucumber and salad with a gooseberry tart or two'.

ENCLOSURE FACTS

❏ After 1750 population growth in Britain increased quickly from 7.6 million to 10.5 million by 1801 – a rapid rise after centuries of slow growth.

❏ Between 1760 and 1793, 1355 parliamentary Enclosure Acts were passed to help increase food production. Six million acres of open fields and common land were enclosed for farming. Northumberland was heavily enclosed because of the importance of the wool industry.

❏ When the feudal system collapsed and the common areas where the peasants had kept livestock, grown crops or hunted rabbits were enclosed by landowners, more and more people became dependent on wages alone which were often fixed at the lowest possible rate.

❏ In Ford most families kept a cow. As many as 70 animals were driven to the common every morning by the village cowherd. This ended with the enclosure of the land causing the villagers' great hardship.

❏ The countryside changed forever. Vast stretches of wild countryside were broken up by hedges, dry stone walling or fences. This new pattern of regular fields with its patchwork of crops and grass is now our familiar landscape.

Forced out: An engraving by Thomas Bewick showing families forced to leave their village because of enclosures

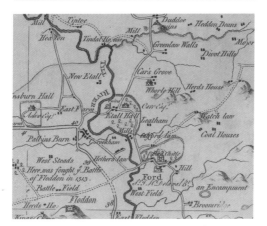

Before enclosures: Armstrong's 1769 map of Ford and Etal

After enclosures: An 1860 Ordnance Survey map showing the new field pattern

Bondage in the fields

Country girl: A watercolour of a woman working in the fields by Louisa Waterford

THEY have been described as looking like romantic milkmaids, evoking images of ruddy-cheeked country lasses wearing ribbons and straw bonnets.

Indeed they were such a striking sight working in the fields around Ford and Etal that travellers to the area often remarked on them, including Beatrix Potter who wrote about them in her diaries.

They were known as bondagers, women who worked on the land, sowing, weeding and harvesting; a distinctive part of the rural landscape of Northumberland and the Borders.

These female workers were part of an ancient system of employment going back hundreds of years.

When a man or 'hind' was hired by a farmer to work on his land, he had to agree to supply a girl for seasonal farm work to pay for the rent for his house.

If the hind did not have a wife, sister or daughter he had to hire a stranger to live with him in his cramped house, usually for a year from May.

It is believed this tradition may date back to a time when men were frequently called to arms and farm labour had to be done by women. Their work would typically include sowing and harvesting turnips, potatoes, hay, corn, planting and maintaining hedging, cutting thistles and filling carts with manure.

They are also mentioned as being well-dressed in their black straw hats lined with red, looking cheerful and healthy while cultivating neat and tidy fields of produce – although this sounds more like a romantic idyll than reality.

But the bondage arrangement provoked controversy. 'Who does not feel for them when out in the midst of a bleak field . . . on damp, drizzly days, with an icy cold wind blowing,' wrote Hastings Neville, rector of Ford in 1897. 'They will probably go on doing this terrible work while the system lasts of which they are a part'.

But this forced employment contract put a strain on crowded poor households and obviously created problems too. There are accounts of illegitimate children, abuse, bondagers being insolent to the hind's wife and resentment at being forced to pay, feed and lodge a stranger.

At its best it allowed girls some independence from their own family and a means of earning their own money. There are records of feisty women striking for higher wages and deriding the amount farmers charged them for beef, mutton, eggs, butter and cheese.

In the 1800s the hinds tried to end the bondage system. It came to a head on a March hiring day in the nearby town of Wooler. A farmer broke rank and hired a hind without the bondage condition. Others did the same. It was the beginning of the end of a centuries-old tradition.

Bondagers: A Victorian photograph showing the women in their distinctive bonnets

THE FARMWORKERS' FLIT

EVERY March farmworkers put themselves up for hire at the local fairs. Wearing a sprig of hawthorn in their hats to advertise their trade, they offered their services to farmers for the next 12 months.

This way of employing farmhands was particularly deep rooted in this area. It had good and bad aspects. The farmer could buy in labour when he needed it. Families wanting work for growing children could change farm. But it meant life was very insecure for many.

As moving day approached nearly every community, school and church was affected. In small hamlets almost half the families would leave at the same time.

One contemporary account describes it as a 'sad day watching the wagons roll up the hills piled high.'

On May 12th, Flitting Day itself, the roads were crowed with workers moving to new farms, belongings piled high on carts often borrowed from their new landlord. Everyone wore their Sunday best clothes.

Towards the end of the 12 months if the farmer didn't engage the farmhand for another year, he and his family had to find a new job and move again.

AN OLD NORSE WORD

THE word flitting is derived from the Old Norse verb *flitten* or *flutten* which means to go away. It was probably introduced into Northumbrian dialect by the Viking settlers.

A similar word *flyttning* is still in use in modern-day Sweden and means move or removal.

Sad day: The flitting from Hay Farm on May 12th about 1900

An industrial heartland

Thriving: An engraving of Ford Forge by John Bailey 1779

Factory to let: Advert for the newly-built forge c. 1769

Still working: Heatherslaw Mill

FORD and Etal once had an industrial heartland with hordes of traffic, swarms of people and constant noise.

From the 1700s around 1,000 people worked on either side of the River Till. There were daily traffic jams as horses and carts lined up waiting to cross the river by bridge, ferry boat or ford.

The right bank of the Till was the manufacturing centre. Ford Forge opened in 1769. It was built by estate owner Sir John Hussey Delaval, who needed a supply of farm tools for his agricultural improvements. The forge also produced mining equipment.

Alongside was a saw mill, a saddler and workshops making bricks, drainpipes and pantiles, which alone employed 80 men.

Wool trade and weaving was also important. On the riverside there was a fulling mill for washing woollen cloth and a carding mill to comb wool ready for spinning.

On the left bank of the river, the water-powered Heatherslaw Mill had been grinding local grain since the 1200s. A well-run mill had always been as important to a country estate as the church and manor house, so farmers could maximise their income.

Etal once had two mills which were also built in the 13th century. But we know little about their hundreds of years of history.

In the late 1700s Ford estate grain was taken to the coast and transported by ship to cities like London.

The mill's slow decline began in the late 1800s with the industrial revolution. Cheaper grain arrived from America and Canada on steamships and was milled at the ports.

The industrial centre suffered too as production and cloth-making was mechanised and moved to the towns.

Years later, in 1975, a charitable trust was set up to restore the crumbling mill to working order and create a museum.

THE MILLER – HIS POWER AND PERKS

GLIMPSES of ladies' bare legs, a cut of every bag of flour, a monopoly of all the estate grain – just a few perks of the miller's job at Heatherslaw.

For he was one of the most powerful men in the community and his mill was the centre of estate life, operating as much like a local trading floor as a place to grind corn. A farmer could borrow money here; speculating against his future commodities such as piglets.

The miller ran a monopoly. Grain grown on the estate had to be milled by him. On top of that he took a cut of every sack of grain, known as an 'moulter', or anything else useful to him or his wife.

Living close by, the miller and his staff worked from dawn to dusk six days a week. As soon as light started to fade, the mill closed. Artificial light was a fire risk, as flammable grain dust swirled everywhere.

This dust had practical uses though. On washdays, when women draped laundry on riverside bushes, the millworkers often threw it out the window. The reason? It forced the girls to hitch their skirts up high to wade into the river and rinse off the dust.

The mill was an important hub in the days before social media. It was here that people met for business.

Once a year, for instance, women came to the mill to sell back their spare grain and made a day of it with a picnic. It was a rare chance to meet and chat.

Millers were among the few literate people and were often called on to read and write letters for estate workers.

The miller kept diaries. These were like 'how to fix it' guides as each mill had its own idiosyncrasies. They were precious and passed down through families.

Many Heatherslaw journals are missing, either lost or destroyed. If a miller was sacked for any reason, he might burn his diaries in front of the estate's agent as a grand gesture of revenge.

Monopoly: An illustration of a miller handing out a sack of flour – an illustration from the Luttrell Psalter. (c) All Rights Reserved. The British Library Board. Licence Number: NOREYE01

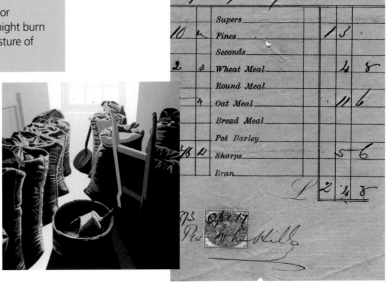

Bill: An 1873 invoice for grain

Hub: The inside workings of Heatherslaw Mill

Coal, carts and rhubarb

MEN and boys have mined coal close to Ford and Etal since medieval times.

Its heyday was during the Victorian industrial revolution and in the 1880s the colliery was as busy as any small town. Around 200 carters a day would transport coal from the Ford Moss pit. They tried to beat the queue by arriving in the early hours.

Those who lived on the roadside were woken in the night by the rumbling of the coal carts.

Inevitably fights broke out as the carters jostled to get in front of the queue. One story tells how a man, who thought he had a right to have his cart at the head of the rank, was dangled over the mouth of the coal shaft until he promised to take his turn.

By 1887 the mine supplied 3,200 tons a year for villages, farms and lime kilns. This was enough work to support around 100 people most of whom lived in a small village next to the colliery.

Around this time there were about 32 cottages around the colliery; most were single-storey with a range for cooking and heating. Families kept pigs and a cow. Water had to be pumped from a nearby well. Women and children brought it home in pails, two at a time using a 'gord' or iron hoop.

There was a blacksmith, stables, a small school, a shop, wells, and an oak-panelled Methodist church which was so cramped many of its services were held outside.

Young boys played on the pit heaps sliding down on sleds. But as soon as they were 12-years-old, they began working deep underground pulling sleds of coal. This work was later done by pit ponies.

However, Ford Moss could not compete with cheaper coal brought to the area by the expanding railway network. The colliery closed in the early 1900s and the village fell swiftly into ruin.

All that now remains of the colliery is the stone-lined mine shafts, the chimney, the engine house and the clumps of rhubarb still growing in what were the old cottage gardens first planted by the miners.

Invoice: The cost of coal in 1872

Colliery life: A miner working underground while (above) a woman carries water from the well

Highlight: An illustration of a 16th century fair from a woodcut by Nikolaus Meldemann

Folklore, football and fighting

AS country life changed over the centuries, folk-lore, old songs and games were abandoned, forgotten or adapted. These are some of them, representing a different age in Ford and Etal's story . . .

Hooligans: Football was an excuse to fight in the 1500s

Prizes: Medals for the winners at the local games

Famous: St Ninian's Fair gingerbread

❏ Football was played in this area as far back as the 1500s. Then the Wardens of the Marches, whose job was to broker disputes between feuding border families, acted as umpires as often the games were just an excuse for the men to fight.

❏ Every September 27th St Ninian's Fair, the social event of the year, took place in an open field. It was a market for sheep, cattle and horses, hardware, cooperage and earthenware. The fair was famous for its gingerbread moulded into Royal Arms, horses and dogs, which was always a popular gift. The fair petered out when the cattle markets moved closer to railway stations.

❏ Every Shrove Tuesday schoolboys in the 1800s were allowed to pay the schoolmaster a penny to watch a cock fight at the Black Bull in Etal. On Palm Sunday the owner of the winner and runner-up birds had to race a mile from church and back again chased by the other boys carrying palm tree branches. If the runners were caught, they were attacked.

❏ Girls came out into the village streets on Easter Tuesday for dancing. Two girls were picked out to dance with each other for as long as they could. The winner was given a pigeon decorated with ribbons.

❏ The Etal Gymnastic Games began in 1836 and were held in the grounds of Etal Manor. Hundreds came to watch shooting, wrestling, and hammer throwing. There were also horse races by the side of the River Till. The farmers rode their own horses so there was fierce competition.

❏ In the 1700s on 'Nutcrock Night', as Halloween was then known, young men stole cabbages and threw them down people's chimneys, often 'with dangerous consequences'.

Love and tragedy. The life of Louisa Waterford

LOUISA Waterford's life reads like a historical romance – a famous beauty and friend of Queen Victoria who tamed and married one of the wildest, richest young men in society. Then tragedy struck.

First, a carriage accident during her honeymoon left Louisa unable to have children and by the age of 40 she was a widow.

Her husband left her the Ford estate and it was here that Louisa fled to grieve and found a distraction from her loneliness, devoting herself to improving the lives of the children and poor.

Within a few years Louisa had created a new village with modern cottages, a reading room, a forge, a dairy, a tea room and a very special school.

Ford village, as we see it today, is the legacy of Louisa's love and loss.

As one contemporary account put it, "Picturesque cottages now line a broad avenue in the centre of which is a fountain with a tall pillar surmounted by an angel. Schools for boys and girls have sprung up . . . it is quite magical."

Louisa was brought up with wealth and privilege. Born in the British Embassy in Paris on April 14th 1818, her father Sir Charles Stuart de Rothesay was a distinguished diplomat.

She and her older sister Charlotte were considered among the most stunning young women of the day and both became friends with Queen Victoria.

Louisa's life seemed even more favoured when, aged 21, she attended that greatest of early Victorian romantic follies, a jousting tournament, and met the immensely rich and wild 3rd Marquis of Waterford, owner of vast tracts of Ireland as well as Ford estate. The attraction was mutual

But, despite his riotous reputation – it's rumoured he once made his horse jump over a dining room table – 28-year-old Henry was too shy to propose and persuaded his sister Sarah to do the job for him.

She wrote a letter to Louisa's mother and the couple married three years later in the Royal Chapel of Whitehall in London in June 1842.

One week after their wedding, 24-year-old Louisa and her new husband were taking a drive around Henry's Irish estate when he lost control of his two horses.

Louisa was knocked unconscious and slipped into a three-day coma. We do not know her exact injuries, but it is thought they would prevent her having the children she longed for.

Letters show the couple were 'devoted' and Henry surprised their families by settling down to married life. For 17 years they lived mostly at his grand family home, Curraghmore in County Waterford. They occasionally visited Ford Castle which Henry had inherited from his mother Susanna, a grand-daughter of Sir John Hussey Delaval.

The wheel of tragedy for Louisa, however, kept on turning. Her beloved husband was killed while he was riding his favourite horse, just a few miles from home, one morning in March 1859. One story suggests he was buried with a twine of his wife's waist-length hair.

Louisa was devastated and later that year she retreated to Ford which Henry left for her to use during her lifetime. There she struggled with her grief. 'There is no part of Ford Castle where I do not see Waterford and hear his voice,' she wrote.

There were more bleak events. During the next six years she lost her sister and mother Elizabeth to both of whom she was very close.

Louisa inherited the family home Highcliffe, a magnificent house in Hampshire, overlooking the Isle of Wight. She started to live at Highcliffe from May to September, returning to Ford in the autumn.

Here, she threw herself into a routine of visiting the poor and sick, helping in the school, singing in the church choir and running a Sunday school.

In many ways Louisa was a modern, pioneering patron, striving to alleviate poverty and assuming some responsibility for the physical comfort and moral well-being of her estate workers.

But we should perhaps also consider that Louisa's

privileged position in life did make it possible for her to be a benevolent lady of the manor and for half the year she was an absentee owner.

As the years passed, Louisa continued to spend her time between her two homes. Her humble nature and slightly hesitant manner meant she had many friends to stay and she was often in London too seeing art exhibitions.

In 1890, however, and now 72, she wrote prophetically, "I feel sadder than usual at leaving Highcliffe this time as if it might be the last visit."

It was. Louisa died peacefully in her bed at Ford Castle early one May morning in 1891. She was buried in the village churchyard. The stone cross, which marks her grave, was designed by her dear friend the celebrity portrait painter George Frederick Watts.

Devoted: Louisa's husband Henry

Retreat: Louisa sought solace at Ford Castle after her husband's death

Famous beauty: An oil painting of Louisa Waterford by Sir F.W. Grant courtesy of The National Portrait Gallery, London

Louisa's passion for painting

PAINTING was a common aristocratic hobby in the 1800s, but Louisa had a talent for art that was admired by everyone from Queen Victoria to the most influential artists of the day.

Her artistic ability had caught the eye of the Pre-Raphaelites, Victorian artists who were inspired by classical myth, medieval chivalry and contemporary social themes.

She was also close to one of the great portrait painters of the day, GF Watts, who was as impressed by her powers as an artist as he was by her beauty.

Louisa had painted since she was a young girl, but developed a love of Italian art during an 18-month grand tour through Europe in 1835, which inspired her to work more seriously. Her own looks beguiled the young Italian artists who begged to paint her.

From then on, her sketch books became a record of her life and travels. Wherever she was, Louisa enjoyed drawing the scenes she saw in her tiny leather-bound sketchbooks. She particularly loved capturing images of children.

Louisa's most famous work was a series of huge Bible scenes which she painted on the walls of her school at Ford. This took her 21 years.

Her work has earned a place in the Tate Gallery's national collection in London. A watercolour she gave to her friend Queen Victoria, *Relentless Time,* is still in the Royal Library at Windsor Castle.

Talent: Louisa captured every aspect of life on her estates

TEMPERANCE, TEA AND THE NEW TESTAMENT

THERE was a religious boom in England during the Victorian age.

Prayers and Bible readings were part of daily life. Most people went to church at least once, if not twice, on a Sunday; a day strictly set aside for moral improvement and serious reading.

Louisa's life was strongly motivated by her faith. She embraced the evangelical Victorian belief in duty, public service and industry as the basis of a religious life. She devoted herself to good causes which were believed would encourage people to help themselves through hard work, thrift and abstinence.

To encourage her estate workers to live a more pious life she enlarged the church and held Sunday school classes. Louisa regularly read extracts from the Bible to the sick and poor. 'She read the whole New Testament three times to one fortunate invalid', noted the local vicar in admiration.

Although in her younger days Louisa liked a glass of wine, in 1873 she became strictly teetotal and a strong supporter of the Temperance movement. Shortly afterwards she closed the village pub the Delaval Arms changing it into a tearoom.

This was not popular with everyone. The *Berwick Journal* commented: "Individuals frequenting this lovely village will learn with regret that it is contemplated to abolish the inn which has existed there for so long."

Devout: A watercolour of a harvest sermon and (above) two little girls in church in 1880

The highs and lows of life in Ford and Etal

IN Victorian England most people still lived in the countryside and Ford and Etal were bustling villages.

Their way of life had not changed for generations. It was a tough existence which we would consider intolerable today.

Working hours were very long. Women washed cleaned, cooked, made butter and cheese, boiled potatoes for their pig. They were responsible for spinning, mending, darning, knitting and even making candles from sheep fat and soap with soda and lime

After a hard day's work, men would come home and start on the vegetable garden to keep their families in food.

Water had to be collected daily from a communal well and up to 10 families shared one or two privies (toilets) at the end of a garden.

Employment opportunities in Ford and Etal at this time included a rabbit catcher, a blacksmith, a policeman and a tailor. Many young girls and men would go into service at Etal Manor or Ford Castle while women would find work as a laundress or dressmaker.

Everything could be bought locally. There was a grocer, a post office, a butcher, a dairy and a milliner selling straw hats for work and best bonnets for Sundays and holidays. It was very busy at Lent when the farm girls spent their wages on the latest fashions.

Country life had its pleasures too. Village social life revolved around the seasons with fairs, markets, agricultural shows and harvest celebrations. There were dances, lectures and tea parties. One year a course of lectures was organised at Ford Forge to fill in the winter evenings.

The arrival of the travelling dance master was a great occasion. He would stay in the area for two or three months teaching dancing for a small fee and organising dances with music by the local fiddlers. At the end of his stay there was a very popular grand ball. 'The tidings of a coming dance stirs them as nothing else will,' observed the rector Hastings Neville.

He also remembers young farm men and women dancing in the fields on warm summer nights trying to escape the watchful eyes of their parents although this, he warned, 'is not to be recommended'.

These though were the final years of a country way of life that had existed for generations.

Cheaper imported food threatened local farming, expanding cities and towns offered better paid jobs and higher standards of living soon changed villages like Ford and Etal forever.

Daily life: Victorian photographs taken on the estates of Ford and Etal

Rural charm, but real poverty

THE rural charm of the two villages hid the grim reality of poverty and squalor endured behind most doors.

Many families lived in one or two bedroom homes with earth floors that were cold, damp and overcrowded.

A report to Glendale Rural District Council in 1897 highlighted the state of cottages at Ford Hill:

"There are 10 cottages, two have two rooms, but the rest have only one. They have lean-tos which let in the rain, the cottages are not spouted so the walls are damp and the two doors are opposite so it makes the houses very cold. There are six people, including children in some of the single room cottages. Drafts, damp and lack of space."

While this is local rector Hastings Neville's account of life inside one Ford home:

"There is the big wash going on one or two days in the week, there is the baking of many large loaves, and above all, the constant boiling of potatoes for the pig . . . And besides, washing and baking and boiling, the cottager's wife has the porridge to make, and the dinners to get ready for the workers when they come in hungry as Esau, and expecting the meal to be ready to a minute.

"And then there are the children, poor things, the baby to be nursed, and the cradle rocked and the lessons of those who go to school to be learnt.

"Certainly; it is a problem the poor of our district have solved for many years, to carry on all the business of living in one inconvenient room, but at what cost to comfort, health and morals."

The rise of the industrialist – Ford and Etal's new landlord

Industrialist: Lord Joicey at his country estate

Ford Castle: Sold for £250,000

A FEUD between two coalmine owners – the aristocratic Earl of Durham and his rival, the self-made James Joicey, highlighted the politically charged times of late Victorian England as new industrialists challenged the gentry for power.

It also signalled the end of a centuries-old way of life at Ford and Etal.

The hostility began during a miners' dispute in the Durham coalfields when James showed some sympathy for the workers' grievances. The Earl of Durham turned to him and said: "I suppose Mr Joicey you would know about these things".

The young industrialist was offended by this slight on his relatively humble background and replied: "One day My Lord, you will pay for that remark".

And Frederick Lambton, the 4th Earl of Durham did. He was forced to sell the famous Lambton collieries to his rival in 1896, who went on to make a fortune as the coal trade boomed.

James, who was made a baron in 1906, then, like many other newly-wealthy Victorian industrialists, used his money to become a landowner. The new Lord Joicey purchased Ford in 1907 for £250,000. It was the first time the estate had ever been sold. He bought Etal, a year later.

When James's second son Hugh married the Earl's daughter Joan in 1921, how the Earl must have reflected on the shifting power from the landed gentry to a new breed – the super-rich.

The Joicey family's rise began in 1838 when James's uncle, also called James, and a partner set up the Joicey mining company in the Durham coalfield.

James, who was born at Tanfield, County Durham, in 1846, joined the family business when he was 18. Three years later he became a partner and the company went on to become one of the largest exporters in Europe.

James became a pivotal northern business figure and was a Member of Parliament for Chester-le-Street.

But success was tempered by tragedy. His young wife Amy died in childbirth in 1881, just a couple of years after their wedding, leaving him with two baby sons. He married again in 1884 and went on to have three more children with his second wife, Marguerite.

James lived at Ford Castle for almost 30 years until his death in 1936, aged 90, leaving the estates of Ford and Etal to his family, who are still the owners.

CHANGING ROLE OF THE LANDOWNER

AS the wealth of Victorian industrialists grew they aspired to join the landed gentry, buying country homes far away from the grit and grime of the cities where they made their money.

Meanwhile the old ties of lord and peasant that had their origins in feudal medieval England were weakening.

As impoverished landowners, suffering from the massive decline in rural industries were forced to sell their estates and the newly-rich snapped them up. The balance of power was slipping away from the old aristocracy in an increasingly egalitarian modern Britain.

Today, whoever owns the land must still play a crucial element in sustaining the rural economy.

For most of us the countryside is a place of leisure, but it provides many with jobs and homes. The modern landowner must maintain the tranquil appeal of an estate while keeping it financially viable.

The emphasis at Ford and Etal is to restore, conserve and manage the countryside and woodland to support the local economy and ensure the sustainability of the estate for future generations.

From coal to country: Lord Joicey, his son Hugh, later the 3rd Lord Joicey and his two grandsons Michael (left) and David (right)

Ford Village – a miserable place until it was moved

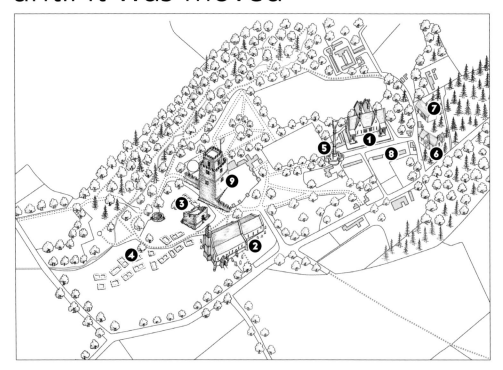

1. Ford School – now Lady Waterford Hall
2. Ford Church
3. Site of ruined Priest's Tower
4. Site of old Ford Village
5. Waterford Memorial
6. Jubilee Cottage
7. Ford Forge
8. New Ford Village
9. Ford Castle

FORD Village was originally huddled around the thick stone walls of the medieval castle under the protective watch of the garrisoned soldiers ready to guard the English borders against the Scots.

For hundreds of years the village stayed in the shadow of the castle stretching down the hill past the church towards the river and bridge. The soldiers, lords and ladies passed by these tiny cottages where some 200 people lived and worked.

It was described as a 'somewhat squalid and miserable place' with a badly paved street and terrible drainage. Like many villages in the Borders it had suffered from lack of investment over the centuries as all money and effort was focused on the battles with Scotland.

In 1859 Ford Castle's new owner Louisa Waterford had the money and a motive to rebuild the village.

Over the next few years the old houses including the vicarage and the top floors of a fortified priest's tower were demolished. A picturesque modern designer village was built on the other side of the castle – out of sight.

The new houses included Jubilee Cottage. It was built in 1887 to commemorate Queen Victoria's Golden Jubilee and was the home of the village nurse. Louisa hired her 'primarily for the benefits of patients of the working classes and for sick poor people'. There were strict rules. She ordered that patients were not allowed to pay the nurse, or offer her food or drink to ensure the poor could afford medical help.

The pretty new cottages, with neat gardens, uniformly set back from the wide streets added to the reputation of the owner, who also now enjoyed beautiful uninterrupted views from the windows of her home towards the Cheviot Hills.

Designer village: Jubilee Cottage (above) and the Waterford Memorial Fountain (below)

Ford Castle

FORD Castle was once a provincial stronghold bristling with armed retainers and for hundreds of years it was a key part of the King of England's border defences.

It has been a medieval manor house, a Tudor castle, a Georgian retreat, a Victorian country home and a special outdoor study centre.

Its first owner Odinel de Ford built a manor house on what was an Anglo-Saxon settlement. When he died in 1276, the estate and house passed by marriage to the Heron family who held it for the next 300 years.

The Herons were given a licence to turn their home into a castle by King Edward III. It suffered heavily during the years of fighting against the Scots and by 1440 it was described as 'the ruined castle of Ford'. Subsequently it was home to prominent families including the Carrs, the Blakes and the Delavals.

It was Sir John Hussey Delaval who invested the then huge sum of £10,500 on a 30-year restoration of the castle from 1760 to 1790 creating a 'useful and noble country seat fit for a lord to entertain his guests'.

When Sir John died in 1808 the castle passed to his granddaughter who had married into the Waterford family of Curraghmore in Ireland. It was inherited by Henry the 3rd Marquis in 1822 and on his death in 1859 his wife Louisa was allowed to keep Ford for her lifetime.

After her death, the Waterfords had no interest in it and sold to the industrialist Lord Joicey.

From 1956 it was used as an outdoor activities centre and thousands of children have stayed here.

Run-down: Ford Castle was in need of repair by the 1700s

CURSE OF THE DELAVALS

THE castle already had a history of feuding and bloodshed when in 1688 it inherited a curse too.

No one knows the origins of the curse, but it warned that if the estates of the Blake family at Ford and the Delavals at Seaton Delaval were ever linked, no man in the family would die peacefully in bed.

It so happened that a young Mary Blake married into the Delaval family and whether it was coincidence or not, there followed a series of bizarre deaths.

Her son Captain Francis Delaval fell down the portico steps at Delaval Hall in 1752 'overweighted by his claret'. He broke his leg and died not long after from complications.

Her grandson, also Francis, racked up £45,000 in debts by drinking, gambling and generally squandering the family fortune. He was found dead, aged 44, in his London lodgings in Dover Street after drinking a bottle of Irish whiskey and gorging on an enormous meal of venison.

His brothers John and Thomas, who renovated Ford Castle, did not escape the curse either. Thomas fell off his horse and died in 1787 while John passed away at his breakfast table in 1808.

Their brothers Robert and Henry lost their lives in battles abroad, George drowned at sea and Ralph was killed in an earthquake in Lisbon.

Then John's only son John was mortally wounded trying to seduce a servant during a trip to the hot springs in Bristol.

Thankfully when the Ford estate passed to the Waterfords it ended the curse.

Ford School

Purpose-built: A school for the village children

WHILE boys and girls have had some education at Ford since the 1700s, the first purpose-built school for village children opened in 1860.

The headmaster's logbooks capture the essence of those Victorian school days with accounts of the Queen's Golden Jubilee races and parties where oranges were a special treat.

We learn that in 1864 and 1865, boys and girls were given new dresses and suits for Christmas so they looked smart when Lady Waterford brought guests to see her modern school. Indeed, the Queen of the Netherlands visited in November 1872 and heard some of the children read. One can imagine how nervous those pupils must have felt.

The daily routine was strict. School started at 9 am and finished at 4.45pm with an hour for lunch. Lessons included arithmetic, grammar, history, geography, sewing, poetry and singing.

Standards were good. A government report for 1869 records: "The order in this school is good. The Religious Knowledge satisfactory and the standard of attainments, generally reflects credit upon the Master's work. The needlework is very fair."

Some of the pupils were models for Louisa Waterford's murals, begun in 1862, which still decorate the schoolroom walls.

The school remained here for almost a century after it opened. It moved in 1957. A charitable trust was then set up to run the building as a village hall and preserve the paintings. It is now known as Lady Waterford Hall.

High standards: A postcard showing the classroom and Louisa Waterford's murals

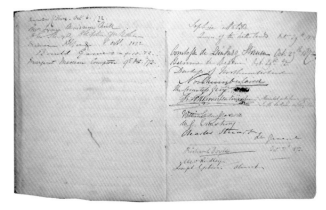

Special guest: The Queen of the Netherlands signed the school visitors' book

Ford Church

History: Ford church about 1870

THE tomb of a knight, a murdered vicar, a raid by the Scots – just a glimpse of the history to be found in Ford Church.

Over centuries St Michael and All Angels has accumulated a wealth of documents and historic items which chart centuries of Ford's past.

Ancient gravestones inside the church relate to a medieval age. A sword and cross mark the death of a knight perhaps in combat, while an engraving of Northumbrian bagpipes suggests the tomb of an armed travelling minstrel who may have stayed at Ford Castle to entertain the lords and ladies.

A wooden panel inscribed with the names of every rector reminds us that parish life was once more turbulent and not just because of the skirmishes with the Scots. In 1575 the then vicar William Bradford was murdered. His patron Robert Carr was arrested for the killing.

Vicars were often sons of gentry and related to their patrons. They took the salary, lived elsewhere and left a curate on a low wage in charge of the parish. In 1760 one vicar had to sign a bond that he would actually live in the parish.

The church records date back to the 1600s. The birth and marriage registers, for example, tell us that most people could not read or write until the 1850s.

Ancient: Medieval gravestones mark the burial places of a knight and a travelling minstrel

Parts of the church were built in the 1200s though most of it was burnt down with the rest of Ford village by Robert Bruce's men in 1314. What was left was restored a century later, but fell into ruin once again in the 1600s.

In 1853 Louisa Waterford, who was then living in Ireland, visited the parish, saw the state of the church and employed the famous architect John Dobson to restore it in fashionable Victorian Gothic style.

Etal Village – comfort for the rich, squalor for the rest

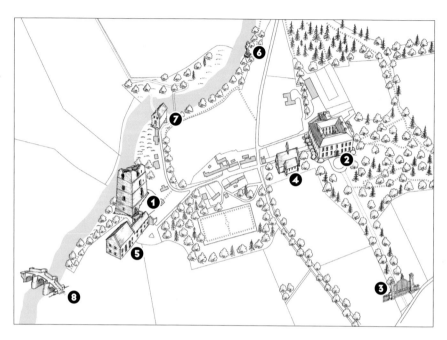

1. Etal Castle
2. Etal Manor
3. Fitzclarence Gates
4. Chapel of Virgin Mary
5. Presbyterian Chapel
6. Ruins of St Mary's Chantry Chapel
7. Site of old mill
8. Site of medieval bridge

ETAL was once a large, lively village protected by the medieval Etal Castle.

It was a thriving community of tradespeople and farmworkers with two corn mills on the riverbank.

The River Till and its medieval bridge was a vital part of village life. Houses, businesses and probably an inn sprang up around this busy crossing. But in the 1500s the bridge was said to have 'decayed and fallen down of late to the great trouble hurt and annuyances of the inhabitants thereabouts'.

No doubt this had an impact on the village's fortunes as did the constant battles with the Scots and neighbouring owners.

The village struggled on, ferryboats replaced the bridge for instance, but there was little inclination to restore or build.

It could still be a lively place for Etal had a thriving religious community. During the 1700s and 1800s hundreds of people flocked to hear the rousing sermons of the influential local preachers at the Presbyterian Chapel

But it was only after the Acts of Union in 1707 united England and Scotland that there was any real stability and investment in Etal.

Reassured by the end of the troubles, 45-year-old Sir William Carr, the owner of the ancient, battered Etal Castle decided it was safe to build himself a comfortable, modern home.

The architect also added a street of picturesque thatched houses, running from his new gates to his old home. They looked pretty, but most were squalid one-bedroom

Vital to the village: The River Till

homes with earth floors. Sir William had no interest in improving the lot of his workers.

In 1827 Etal had 50 houses and 207 villagers; there were two schools, a dairy and a chapel. But little was done to improve living conditions until the early 20th century when the estate was modernised.

Etal
Castle

THIS was the home of Etal's feudal lords for 700 years.

Earliest records show the influential Manners family lived here from 1250. They were permanently at war with the Scots or feuding with their neighbours at Ford.

In 1341 the manor house was granted a licence to become a castle. Its fortunes went up and down over the next hundred years as fighting destroyed the building and the family coffers.

The castle was used as a garrison and was destroyed before the Battle of Flodden. There was no cash to make it habitable and it ended up being used for storage for many years.

The estate passed to the barony of Roos through marriage in 1495. They rented it out before swapping it with the Crown for other lands. It became a garrison for 300 soldiers, which must have had quite an impact on the village.

After the union of the Scottish and English Crowns in 1603, it was decommissioned and the castle was given to Lord Hume of Berwick and then to the Earl of Suffolk.

During the reign of Charles I, Robert Carr bought and restored the estate. When his son William moved to the manor, the castle was never lived in again, but the ruins have been preserved.

In ruins: Etal Castle was destroyed during centuries of fighting

ST MARY'S CHANTRY CHAPEL

IN the early 1300s the Manners family of Etal Castle paid for a private chapel on their land. Chantries were built and funded by private individuals who paid a priest to sing masses for the souls of their dead.

During the reformation in 1545, Henry VIII declared that all chantries belonged to the king. Two years later, his successor Edward VI went further and shut down all 2,374 chantries.

We do not know the exact date when Etal's chantry was closed, but it would have been a significant loss to the village. Chantry priests frequently served their community by offering some education to the poor.

EL.16F   THE MANOR, ETAL

A splendid family home: Etal Manor

Etal Manor

BUILT by Sir William Carr in 1748, the manor passed
through marriage to the Boyles, the Earls of Glasgow.
It was loaned to Lord Frederick Fitzclarence when he
married Lady Augusta Boyle and they moved into the
manor in 1821.

Lady Augusta was widowed in 1854 and lived at Etal
until her death. In 1876 the house reverted back to the
Earls of Glasgow. They sold the estate to Sunderland
shipbuilder Sir James Laing in 1885.

It changed hands again when Durham coal owner
Lord Joicey, who already owned Ford, bought the estate
in 1908. During the First World War, the house was
loaned to the army for convalescing soldiers. After
1921 it became a family home once more.

Lord Frederick Fitzclarence

THE illegitimate son of a king and an actress, Lord
Frederick Fitzclarence, who lived at Etal Manor, was a
man of dubious moral values.

This led him into conflict with the up-standing but
outspoken village preacher the Reverend Aitken.

When Lord Fitzclarence threatened to turf out
his estate workers and demolish their cottages, the
Reverend Aitken embarrassed him by preaching from
his pulpit in fiery tones about cruelty and injustice.
The arrogant lord, whose father became William IV,
was forced to back down.

The Fitzclarence Gates

THE story is that these huge ornate gates have never been opened.

They were commissioned by Lady Augusta as a surprise for her husband who was serving in India with the British Army. But Lord Frederick died of an illness at Poona in 1854 and never saw his gift. His embalmed body was brought back home to be buried. His bereft wife could not bear to use the new entrance and by tradition they remain closed.

The illegitimate son of a king: Lord Frederick Fitzclarence painted by Richard Barrett Davis

Closed: The love gift that Sir Frederick never saw

The Chapel of The Blessed Virgin Mary

Etal: The Chapel of The Blessed Virgin Mary

Grieving for her only child and her husband, who died within a year of each other, Lady Augusta commissioned a chapel to be built in her garden in 1856. Two years later Augusta's daughter Frederica and husband Frederick were exhumed and buried in its vaults.

The chapel was designed by the famous Victorian architect William Butterfield, whose work includes Keble College, Oxford.

Bibliography

J. Thompson, D. Wood and A. Sparke, *Ford Castle*, Shiel & Morrison: Berwick-upon-Tweed (1977)

Frank Graham, *Wooler, Ford, Chillingham and The Cheviots*, Frank Graham: Newcastle upon Tyne (1976)

R. Gill, 'Priest and Patron in a Northumberland Parish' in *A Social History Of The Diocese Of Newcastle*, W.S.F. Pickering, ed. Oriel Press: Stocksfield, Northumberland (1981)

M. Girouard, *The Victorian Country House*, Yale University Press: New Haven and London (1985)

James Joicey ed., *Ford At The Time of the Waterfords 1822-1907*, Northumberland County Library: Morpeth (1992)

Michael Joicey, *Louisa Anne Marchioness of Waterford,* The Trustees of The Lady Waterford Hall: Ford, Northumberland (1991)

M. Lynch, *Scotland A New History*, Century Ltd: London (1991)

I. Donnachie and G.A. Hewitt, *Companion To Scottish History,* B.T. Batsford: London (1989)

Hastings Neville, *A Corner in the North: Yesterday and Today with Border Folk*, Andrew Reid & Co Ltd: Newcastle upon Tyne (1909)

Hastings Neville, *Under a Border Tower*, Mawson, Swan & Morgan: Newcastle upon Tyne (1897)

S. Scott, *Glimpses of Ford*, Shiel & Morrison: Berwick-upon-Tweed (1992)

Stan Beckensall, *The Prehistoric Carved Rocks of Northumberland*, Frank Graham: Newcastle upon Tyne (1974)

A.D. Mazel, G. Nash, C.Waddington, *Art as Metaphor: The Prehistoric Rock-Art of Britain,* Oxford: Archaeopress (2007)

Northumberland Rock Art: Web Access to the Beckensall Archive (http://rockart.ncl.ac.uk)

George MacDonald Fraser, *The Steel Bonnets*, Harper Collins: London (1995)

The Gefrin Trust, *Yeavering: Rediscovering the Landscape of the Northumbrian Kings,* Northumberland County Council: Morpeth *(2009),*

Barbara Bryant, *GF Watts Portraits Fame and Beauty in Victorian Society*, National Portrait Gallery: London (2004)

Morris Bishop, *The Pelican Book of the Middle Ages*, Pelican Books: Harmondsworth, Middlesex (1983)

Jane Lyell, *The Battle of Flodden September 9th 1513,* Shiel & Morrison: Berwick-upon-Tweed.

C.P. Hill, *British Economic and Social History 1700-1982*, Edward Arnold: London (1986)

Christopher Lee, *This Sceptred Isle 55BC-1901,* Penguin Books: London (1998)

G.E. Mingay, *Rural Life in Victorian England*, Alan Sutton: Stroud, Gloucestershire (1990)

Asa Briggs, *A Social History of England*, Penguin Books: Harmondsworth, Middlesex (1985)

J. Bailey and G. Culley, *Agriculture of Northumberland, Cumberland and Westmorland*, Frank Graham: Newcastle upon Tyne (1972)

The Monthly Chronicle of North-County Lore and Legend, vol v. No 47, Walter Scott: Newcastle upon Tyne (January 1891)